AF446767
AF446767

PURSUITS

PURSUITS

By

Laurence W. Thomas

THE GOLDEN QUILL PRESS
Publishers
Francestown · New Hampshire

Library of Congress Catalog Card Number 86-81930

ISBN 0-8233-0427-2

Printed in the United States of America

CONTENTS

FOREWORD

Pursuit is our never-ending endeavor, reaching towards unsatisfying goals which, even when surpassed, are still sought. Pursuit alone provides challenges which fulfill, challenges based on finding ourselves in a time span called life and needing to do something with it. Necessary pursuits include satisfying our most basic need: survival. With and beyond that, sequences of events fill our time, happening in some place. We perpetuate our kind holding on to dreams celebrated with the coupling of two lives and bodies. We educate ourselves, seeking bare truth, regarded, considered, accepted, rejected, groping for realization and fulfillment, a vision of a world to build.

Most pursuits we invent. Law, art, myth and religion, and the uses of nature comprise man-made codes; we thrive on complicating them and are exercized at their abuse. We start small, cultivating and domesticating for our own uses, expanding our caves into metropolises, reordering nature into forms unrecognizable, ending up masters of god and man and nature.

Pursuits are necessary; we must always be doing something with our days. Whether it be contriving to look occupied or choosing between amusements, we head in counter directions. We dig into our pasts seeking to gain, to preserve what memories serve inaccurately and depending on writ to justify our autonomous self-interest. Individual pursuits of the present are largely hedonistic. We reflect on the future, with much emphasis laid on unprovable and unsupportable prophecy.

The pursuits declared for us by Jefferson seem elusive. Life continues to be argued inconclusively, liberty taken for granted until challenged, and happiness is lost simply through failure to recognize it. We are constantly subjected to pressures from all sides—advertisements telling us our condition is far from replete, religions insisting that other worlds are more desirable, organized labor cultivating discontent, entertainers and the media inflicting their standards upon us, professionals insinuating themselves into positions of indispensability, politicians inflating their power to control all aspects of our lives—pressures so all-pervasive and constant that the greatest right, the right of individual identity, has been all but obliterated.

From among these threads I have chosen themes, loosely weaving them into the fabric of *Pursuits*.

I. PURSUIT OF THE WHOLE

PURSUIT OF THE WHOLE

Among habituees approaching
Vauntingly, diffidently,
Those purposeful and initiated,
Scheming and skillful,
Or those less assertive,
Reticent but receptive,
One hesitates, pauses
Irresolutely at the threshold,
Surveys, tense, unfamiliar,
Sensing certain threat and welcome,
A knowledge that unawakened feelings
Are not new, recalling moments
Suppressed but relevant,
Sentiments unexplored but component,
Emotions stirring but remaining latent,
Unused quarters
Seen to be exploited.

Doors creak open,
Bang shut,
As layers of pretense
And sophistication removed
Reveal bare truth,
Regarded, considered,
Accepted or rejected
In the eyes of expert
Adjudicators and apprentices alike,
Well-equipped
Vying with emergent,

Strengths and weaknesses
Noted and compared,
Seekers groping
For realization and fulfillment
In fetid cloister
And steamy sanctum.

Reduced to pristine nakedness
In the unrelenting light
Of inspection and introspection,
External differentiations
Are shed to expose underlying
Valid distinctions and values,
A critical sense
Developing along with systems
Of adequate action and reaction,
Standards evolving.

Exposure and association,
Inundation and absorption,
Lead one gradually
But inexorably
Beyond edges of awareness,
Through expanding atmospheres
Of apprehension and enlightenment
To broadened concepts
Couched in security,
Inner confidence,
Loss of innocence,
And self-fulfillment.

THE TRUE AMERICAN

There were no mirrors
and only frontiers established,
broken by the true American and
not reflecting on the nonexistent
he forged forward
in the one direction visible
soon discovering that
frontiers end within himself
and individualism allies itself
with autonomous self interest.
Progress is an accident of fits
and starts only with a need
to occupy a void, to fill
available emptiness with the
passionate pursuit of
self gratification.
In greed-shattered dream he moved,
learned the liberty
not to exercize his freedoms,
the paradox of practicing them
too much. He moved rootless
searching for a soul
he could not find without
looking into another soul
or with thorough inward
contemplation of himself, but
there were no mirrors
and only frontiers established,
broken.

MINORITIES

They lurk, alert, afraid of shadows
Under umbrageous camouflage,
The night, their mentor, their accuser,
A protection from injustice,
Pontificating on their faults,
The day, productive,
A time for them to hide
Like tapped turtles, asexual
And remote.

They seek safe places,
And their selves,
Of necessity for survival, and
Retreat behind absurd disguises
Fitted to accommodation.

Lost in the trappings,
The deceits, gaining from them
The genius for achievement and damnation,
Still they emerge from their cocoons
Like viceroys who mimic monarchs
With outward, self-preserving aping,
Do not deviate from their assigned positions,
Still accomplish their own and nature's missions.

They have found
An independence of the mind
Against the material world imposed
On which they still depend,
A victory won by the mind from matter,
Their enemy, their friend.

DISSERTATION ON A WHITE FENCE

Hung on pins like calendar appointments, past
and yet to come,
like life it rises from the sea
(like life there disappearing) to run its course
of our experiences. Swimming into consciences,
its history, ours, dimmed by distances
too misted for memory, too fogged to foresee.

Momentarily focused on segments and sequences,
the fence wanders on, interlinking our histories,
futures, not dividing, like walls
in Berlin or in China; we learn that good neighbors
make good fences, the chain broken only
by our lack of objective perspective.

Two thousand panels
mirror years of accomplishment,
reflect on the future, aired, viewed
for a moment
but permanence isn't an issue.
No voices and trumpets sound, ending its vigil
and though gone, still it lingers
photographic in memory, heading prophetically
into fulfillment, oblivion.

CITY AWAY

Arrival awakens this dawning city
Aging away from passing the time,
Renewal gaining from ravage respected as
Custom: tranquility balances yearning.

Discovery enriches this welcome city
Escaping indifference to unwonted attentions;
Meandering garden paths passing fountains
Mix with tradition, beauty, utility.

Thought enlightens this sunset city
Settling away from shocks and monotonies.
Clouds fold down over edges of mountains
Before they dissolve to complete apprehension.

Comfort shelters this winter city
Waiting warmly away from nonentity,
Gently enfolded in the palm of the mountain
Surrounding, safe in its craggy enclosure.

SIREN SONG

When young Ulysses heard the sirens'
Treacherous singing, he had reason
To rejoice; courting danger, even wide awake
To jeopardy, rarely goes
Unpunished, but he was wont to sleep

In peril, and in horses, ending wars. Reason
Sits aloof from conflicts, puts to sleep
Offending causes and effects the silencing of sirens.
Accord is lost, leaving in its wake
Distrust, misunderstanding, when the envoy goes

Away because he is disinclined to reason
At the conference table. The U.N. sleeps
Its usefulness away and still the sirens
Sound their warnings, and innocents awake
To wonder how the battle goes.

Flashing lights, horns, bells, sirens
Alert those not involved to catastrophe, wake
Benighted senses to dilemma, give reason
To count blessings as the saying goes
And turn to restless, troubled sleep.

Prepared for, trouble often goes
Before it starts, giving way to reason
Through the safeguard of being awake.

Though they disobeyed him, his men were not asleep
When young Ulysses heard the sirens.

When sirens awake reason goes to sleep.

EPITAPH FOR A NURSEMAID

Belike the transformation came
To thousands like her,
Sudden, irremediable,
A distant rumble or a speck on the horizon
Considered or ignored,
Welcomed with uncomprehending deference
And regarded as
Nothing so very revolutionary.

It really was no change at all,
Except in names alone, for them
And her, of course, who died.
Distantly she watched, remotely
Over fences, perhaps, or in parks
Discussed with vaguest apprehension,
But she had her place
However much they struggled
Over ideologies and who would hire the nursemaids.

And so she died, a symbol,
Not for causes and overwhelming reforms
But because to get a perambulator
From the upper town
One must descend broad steps
With care,
To the proletarian dockyards.

(In Eisenstein's film, *The Battleship Potemkin*, a nursemaid
with a perambulator was killed on the Odessa Steps, caught
in a revolutionary situation.)

"MINE IRONY SURPASSETH ALL OTHERS"
Death, in *The Temptation of Saint Anthony*

Consider, then.
Pride and pageantry
When prime ministers and princes pass,
Convulsions of impassioned rapture
Attend departure of low or lofty
From single passing bell
To extermination of races.
Consider pomp and circumstance,
Ceremonies, celebrations
Attendant on the wonderwork of
Raging war: martial music
And high masses. Saints are made
And heroes too, perpetuating
The savagery of cemeteries,
The nobility of names engraved.
Consider these, O
San Antonio!

WERE IT NOT FOR DEATH

Stand aghast at horrors, and fears
Like ignorance will creep and conquer,
Culminating in the use of force

Which settles nothing. Ours
Is to question, not to suffer
From our inadequacies, wars

Of our devising, or theirs
With whom we differ
And brutishly contend. Where is

The victory when bellicose ideas
Are not abolished in the victor
Nor the vanquished? What conquers

Must be conquered from within: the powers
Of death and ignorance, for
Were it not for death, there would be no wars.

LIBERATION

Are these not the children flying now
In their shattered street around a pole
Who yesterday were stealing tattered
Through their street resentful and afraid,
Their hunger gnawing with a rusting blade
These aging ladies?

Was their game today not played before—
An outgrowth of their need to celebrate
And soar above their battered street—not played
From joy but fear of what is circling below
These ancient ladies?

And do they know the games that other children play
Along their scattered streets, choosing sides
And playing at a game of tag or war,
Or is only swinging round a pole amusing for
These dying ladies?

THE LUCKY DRAGON

The men of science turn the golden page.
The fishers leave to cultivate the sea.
Sing loud the coming of the peaceful age.

The Lucky Dragon clears the harbor to engage
In age-old harvest action; as they flee,
The men of science turn the golden page.

The other dragon roams the islands in a rage,
Lays eggs, so in their final hatching, we
Sing loud the coming of the peaceful age.

The Lucky Dragon's sailors disengage
Their engines off Bikini, do not see
The men of science turn the golden page.

The other dragon, restive in its cage,
Struggles, suddenly emerges, and is free.
Sing loud the coming of the peaceful age.

The meeting of the dragons sets the stage
Where scientists and fishermen agree
The men of science turn the golden page;
Sing loud the coming of the peaceful age.

(The Japanese fishing boat, *The Lucky Dragon*, was caught in the fallout of the atomic test on Bikini and the fishermen were killed.)

TERRORISM

Order justifies itself
And all these petty irritations—
   bombs at midnight
   the deaths of innocents
Deny what gratifies
The vulgar in their lack of apprehension,
Their orderly acceptance
Of existing satisfactions—
Attacking dim awareness
With what they cannot know.

A law is never wrong
Which is enforced;
It may be wrong for
Other places, other times.
A missionary in a desert land
Has ineluctable questions he must face:
Does he have something practicable to replace
That which he destroys—and
Will it not work better in another place?
He should go there
Rather than to suffer futile fate
(an insignificant death serves little)
And accomplish nothing through infinitesimal protest:
   Even in a fascist state
   What serves most serves best.

THE DISPOSSESSED

They saved whatever they could,
The dispossessed—their home
In ruins, village gone—
They saved few things
Besides themselves
With value only
To their owners:
    You cannot sell
    However rich your blood
    Ancestral portraits
    And survive in camps.
    Who needs
    With villages like yours
    Proliferating throughout the world
    The burden of another child?

EVEN ON CHRISTMAS

They didn't know the season,
Those who left their homes
Not for shopping in tinsel and lights
With carols broadcast
Or for visiting grandmother;
They took her with them
If they could. Their tinsel
Was barbed, and their only light—
A rocket flare
Hanging in the East.

LE QUATTRO STAGIONI

L'Autumno

In summer and autumn August
Seasoned armies
Of soft airs, gentle nights
And football players
Infiltrate
To battle over weather predictions
And harvest report.

September sings triumphant,
Rallies and retreats,
Surrenders back to school
And office hours and leaves
Late vacationers to retire
From empty beach
To fireside friendships
Cabined as a last resort.

From a sister summer
Flickers hope remaining,
Mingles arguments with boredom
And anxiety, then relinquishes all
Before the threat of winter and
Readily accepts the fall.

LE QUATTRO STAGIONI

L'Estate

    Lhude sing
At last anticipated summer
Time of sojourn and sunburn,
Lewdly pursuing bikini and short
Necessary cash to realize
Pipe and winter dreams
Of well-earned vacations.

    Sing too
Reuniting families, summer camp,
A backyard barbecue with
Unwelcomed mosquitoes and neighbors,
Chances to retreat
Down dusty byways
With multitudes of others
Escaping cities' heat.

    Sing
Ball parks, picnic sites, fair grounds
For illegitimate wishes
Of expeditiously returning to
The normalcy of autumn.
    Sing cuccu!

LE QUATTRO STAGIONI

La Primavera

The rights of rain
With all responsibilities
Which pertain thereto begin
With blizzards' equivocal eviction
And fancies lightly turn
To thoughts of love, spring
Training and the seed catalogue.

With bleat or roar
March's departure
Signals the advent of April,
Makes way for the fragrance
Of burgeoning earth
Flourishing verdancy and
Ubiquitous persistence of drizzle.

Shut-ins of winter
Warming to welcome weather
Hailing bud and sprout
Emerging, go out to greet
The season urging truancy,
House cleaning, home repairs and,
With summer still ahead
The heat.

LE QUATTRO STAGIONI

L'Inverno

    Conversations
Circumnavigate the world
Of ice conditions, hockey
Weather and the price of coffee,
Accompany all adjustments
As man prepares
To meet in combat
Man bedecked in trappings
That transform the issue
From frosty friendships
Of a summer dream to
Shin guards, sticks, and
Puck admonishing what fools we be
To abate the battle
Till we have blown our noses.

    Wary at first
Of summer joints
And creaking forth
Avoiding falls and winter's
Grasp when fancies
Never turn but lightly
Come admiring, we flash past
The lusty men desiring
And waiting out their fate
To cut a figure eight.
    Soon retiring.

II. PURSUIT OF THE MYTH

OUTWORN MYTHS

What myths wear out
Still stimulate
Those who discover in the gods
Acts unqualified, still
Stir imaginations to step outside
What fears and hopes
And learning teach,
To see communication
Relevant and unpresuming. Alibis
Contemporary or otherwise
Exist without evasion
Of responsibility. Myths can mirror
And not exclude
The artists' implications,
And courage, too, requires
Both vision and reflection.

FATE AND THE ANGEL OF DEATH

Have we not probed the haunts, the hidden niches
In our relentless search for the inexorable spinner
That she may profit from practical application
Of our better methods and materials?

Is not her endlessly measuring self sought
Unceasingly by science to be schooled
In the benefits of quality control and doubled
    production?

Does not persistence continue to include
Descrial of that daughter of destiny with sharp shears
To show actuarial advantages of avoiding wasted
    action?

Still, indeterminately she hesitates,
Equivocates, loyal to her old employer
Who rigidly refuses reversal of reliance
On his antiquated system of accounts.

And still the sun shines ironically on an interminable
    world
Where paradoxically everything is ephemeral.

ST. MARTIN AND THE BEGGAR

How great a Christian charity
To cleave the superabundant robe
Which of your rank speaks little.
This pristine nakedness
And adulate glance
Confide to mystic origins
Which you by such benevolence
Aspire to acquire.
There is in his pure aspect
A communion of desire
Which transcends the beggar state
Understanding your nobility
Sharing nobleness itself.
And you by your compassioned gesture
Are recompensed without attaint
For he becomes the giver
And you become a saint.

MARY AT THE MANGER

Crouched in faithless
Inconsiderate mingling
Of cattle and asses,
Waiting to be delivered
Of a burden
She cannot account for,
Mary moans in holy horror
Of the preconception—
That struggling, kicking
New idea—old already
At its birth.
Joseph coughs
And looks apologetic.
Visitors misguided
By the tongues of angels,
Finding nothing to fulfill
Their hopes for gain
Nor answers to mysteries
As cattle low
And shepherds flock
To see the magnificence of kings,
Depart in disappointment.

CASTAWAYS

Still indispensable,
Things useful, needed,
Are never hung on poles
And those who nail them there
With eyes only for
Casting lots
Away
Satisfy aesthetic need
And purpose practical
Someplace else,
Make living room
For essential, useful things, and
Hang the rest in otiose
Junkyards of the soul.

EL SEMBRADOR

The sower turns his back upon his seeds;
He cannot tell the flowers from the weeds.
The fruitless must be nurtured with the fruit.

The bad is planted by some evil doer.
As weeds proliferate, the plants are fewer.
The garden is entangled in a plot.

The reapers choose the good and burn the weeds.
Fruition is the test of what succeeds.
Productive plants survive among the tares.

Love, birth and death, suspicions, trust, mature.
Ugliness and beauty both endure.
Productive plants survive among the tares.

They grow together, flowers and the weeds:
Results of both good planting and misdeeds.
The garden is entangled in a plot.

Seedlings look alike until mature.
Unproductive plants will die, the good endure.
The fruitless must be nurtured with the fruit.

"MAN'S WOLF TO MAN"

Reducing ourselves to the animal levels
Is not wasteful; unthinking nature reworks
Its materials, tearing down to rebuild
From its limited stockpile, reusing
The stuff of destruction. The replication
Is what is important as
Nature and man compete to produce
Original creations repeated from patterns
Multitudinously various in the cases of nature,
But with man attained with monotony.

Notably few advances mark progress
Since the Greek golden era, electricity
Notwithstanding or flush toilets.
We know more than Socrates:
History, however, still being measured
In wars and destruction, our
Efforts today are not towards advancement
But how to stave off extinction.

We don't think, so we aren't
Any more than the beasts and we head
In counter directions. We have lost
What we gained when Jesus preached healing
And Plato spoke to Thoreau.

IN PRAISE OF SINNING

There are, of course, more than seven
Times seven as we would be convinced
By those who at random create them,
From inventions such as Eve and Prometheus
To their perpetuation by mass media
And organized labor. They proliferate,
Both sin and virtue, with unclear demarcation,
Overlapping, dependent one upon the other
For continuing success, the question of merit
Left hanging in some doubt.

Those equivocally termed deadly,
Whether sins or virtues, hang dilemmatically
In the balance depending on how they're regarded.
We give millions to missions
Whose religious intention is
Teaching us how we should think
And with ignorance stick with traditions
Unthinking, mistakenly linking that which has passed
With the good. This is bad
And leaves liberals taking advantage
Of those not inclined to be sensible.
The fault is resultant in excesses
Dragging us into the sins of psychiatry,
Labor-saving inventions, lip-service liberation
Of women and other useful minorities, and the
Primitive persistence of grave yards.

We should be pleased with the satisfactory
Outcome of endeavors, understanding
That pride can produce other than failure,
Competitive envy is useful, lust productive,
Sloth regenerative, gluttony fulfilling,
Anger self-protective, and avarice
Leads to advancement.

HAST THOU NEVER LOVED A VIRGIN?
—Lust, in *The Temptation of Saint Anthony*

What tremors of pleasure attend
The tentative coupling of warm hands,
Exploration of eyes exchanging
Apprehension and acquiescence.
Envision sweet images of surrender,
The passing of remorse in tears,
In the wood, under the moon.
As two hearts join, fill, burst
In a whirl of eddying passion,
Such an overflowing of intoxication
That you will wish to press
The whole world against your heart
With love!

"LAUGH NOW, HANDSOME HERMIT, LAUGH!"
—The Queen of Sheba in
The Temptation of Saint Anthony

Place but a finger upon my shoulder
To feel a stream of fire course through your veins.
Ecstasy greater than owning empires
Attends possession of the least part of me.
My kisses have the taste of fruit.
What will you have? A woman of passion
With a sensual voice and lusty form,
Flaming hair and superabundant flesh?
Do you prefer a body cold as a serpent's skin,
Solid but responding? Behold these eyes,
Deeper, more inscrutable than caverns—
Look into them. I am not a woman;
I am a world.

"RESIST NOW! I AM THE OMNIPOTENT!"
—Lust, in *The Temptation of Saint Anthony*

Bethink yourself
Of pious resolution, courageous course,
Virtues, patience, restraints, ambitions
All dissolving in that sweet scent
Of lustful resignation and pursuit,
Engendered for death's ultimate destruction,
Equal in rage, greater in violence.
For I, too, scream and kick,
Have sweats and agonies and
Aspects cadaverous, but
Unlike Death, I am hungered after
At every step man takes, even
From the threshold of the tomb, for
I give promise of appeasement, fulfilling
All desire beyond conception.
Bethink yourself of this,
Unhappy hermit.

FRUSTRATION

The zoo was crowded that day
And I hadn't shaved.
Two seals lay looking like two
Old men in bed, with which
Observation I was shocking my friend
When our eyes met. I stared
Too long and scared
The glance away and
The brown seal barked
In anger at not being able
To rest his head on the tan seal.
I looked again and there it was
But more shy, wary of eagerness
And more interested in the
Spider monkeys. The bison smelled.
The deer smelled.
The hippopotamus lay half
Submerged in dirty water.
Only one sad-eyed bird
Sat still and the bird house
Smelled and was crowded that day
And I hadn't shaved.

THE DISILLUSIONED

They laughed their lives
And scoffed the inauspiciousness
    Accomplishing what all men do,
    No more.
              Memories are light and fade—
Frail things to rely upon—
              And now
They mourn a tolerable fate,
And cannot fulminate against
A world they did not touch.

They cannot hunger much.

ENNUI

Then, the mind and flesh responded to
Temptations, mere alternatives arrayed
For choosing between amusements
Parading in profusion with hardly time
For pleasures crowding round the clock
Like guests at a reception.

                      Now,
The gates of the mind swing inward
And irresponsive body binds the soul
To memories gathering at the stopped clock
Like mourners at a wake
Waiting vainly for manifestations of miracles.

OBITUARY

On that priestly lettered journey
to Damascus, the bus broke down
and we alone continued to the house
in Straight. I, too, was going to be
a teacher and took the job with him
because the pay seemed good. And there
we lived and moved and had our
breakfasts served in bed.

Invited East for lectures,
we argued too much
and were suspect,
open to interpretations
which threatened our convictions.
It wasn't always easy,
sharing travel, and accommodation
sometimes irritating and inadequate.

Trouble started over Mark,
who traveled with us,
since with three together
one, somehow, feels left out,
so after sharp contention,
we parted company, he
to visit Europe, we
deciding on an insular retreat.

Somewhere I must have kept his letters
written as the spirit moved
from Rome and Athens,
postcards of the Acropolis, accounts
of getting stoned and various affairs,
letters of love and admonitions
that we should share
our lives in peace. And when he died
I didn't know about it. I could have
sold the letters.

Glorify thyself
Among kings and saints,
Virgins, confessors and patricians
Who all found glory and fulfillment
In self-inflicted death. Think!
Destroy the potter's work,
Become greater than the clay—
Equal to the one who works it.
Deny the body that so mocks the mind
And in vengeance find release
From its encagement. Courage
Will be rewarded in heights,
Not depths, and thou cannot
Suffer much. What is there
For thee to fear?

SELF RELIANCE

Committed to suicide or public display
For peevish irritability or exacerbated pride?
The brutal world, fundamentally indifferent,
Turns its face of insufferable condescension,
Mocks and flatters with appalling insensitivity,
A complete negation which conquers the conscience.
Activity answers, lamentations only ask,
Shrugging off instead of shouldering responsibilities,
Laying blame for lack of attainment
On the conscience of the generation,
The accumulations of the past. The ego is now
And entirely inward, composed of responses
To physique and mentality shaped to environment,
Existence defining the essence.

THE END OF DREAMS

Wistfully, fingers unfurl along edges,
Curl around corners, appraising
The value of treasures and visions,
Caressing here curtains, there
Recollections, assessing the contents
Of cupboards and prospects,
Prompted by envious urgings.

Alarmingly, tongues lash out
Finding fuel for their arguments,
Licking at pictures,
Laughing at luxuries, leaping
From bed to conclusion.
Things loved too much perish
And a dream becomes just an illusion.

AFTER RAIN

After rain, the desert's usual umber
Shifts to delicate shades of dusty green,
Lavender and pale pink appearing
Between the thorns of more
Enduring denizens. Flowers form from
Sleeping things, dormant but not dead,
Celebrating seasons, from seeds
And bulbs and roots waiting to be waked
By water and warm sun, waiting
With the animals for birth, immortal
As anything we will ever know.

IMMORTALITY

When old man Pinzon passes on,
He won't just cease; he'll be remembered
For weeks by the worms, a generation
Of much obliged microbes, and anyone else
Who bothers to notice his tombstone,
No more than a pause in the graveyard.
His family will always recall him,
Seeing themselves in their mirrors,
As not fat but quite pleasingly
Obese, and his features
Will survive as those of his offspring.
Affection and discipline lavished in life
Will outlast him as long as the living
Recall them or according to their lights
Allow them a place in their lifestyles.
His bequest to posterity
Will include his apartment
(rent paid to the end of the month),
An overtaxed income and furniture,
For a time enough to survive on,
And a few weeks' employment for tailors.
He will leave as his legacy
His quips and his teases,
La Familia Pinzon drawn by an innocent artist,
And the musings of one minor poet.

III. PURSUIT OF ONE OR ANOTHER

RITES OF SPRING

Go down with me now,
down before grasses green, before mandragora
rootlets swell to proportions beyond ecstasy,
beyond encompassment, perfusion. Go
down, together, now when green
forthcomes, when green impends,
foretokens profuse fulfillment;
green promises, stimulated, excitation.
Ferns, now just fiddleheads unfurl,
still succulent. Now creepers reach
with tentative tendrils, caress tenderly
trunks of trees with bare branches
shadowless except for traceries
nakedly embroidered on carpets of leaves.

Now you must go with me,
now among mushroom caps ready to swell,
touched with faint dampness, dew droplets
of fresh morning's taste, subtle as nectar
that overflows like milky warm light aslant
through young branches and stirs dormant juices
to circulate systems, to issue through stems,
vines, veins all atingle in anticipation
as sun fingers stroke young stalks
so sap rises to burst buds
on branches extending. Now arbutus seduces,
bedded in blankets of needles, under covers
of leaves while violet's breath teases.

Watch with me now young lilies emerge.
Linger alongside languid rivulets
with redbuds reflected in pristine nubility
underneath skies of pale blue enticement
lightly painted in finger curl clouds
that beckon, bird flights that lure.
Go with me now to the woods.

THE KISS

We learn young and then too soon forget
About aggressiveness in our world
Of boundaries that should not be transgressed
But often are. We learn young,
Too soon capitulating to forces
Once eschewed with innocent instincts,
Too soon neglecting warnings
Infused in dimmest infancy,
Dim instinctive warnings that neglected
Upset what we learn young
And then too soon forget.

OUR KNEES TOUCHED

Our knees touched—
not the knees that quake
halfway between quivering feet
and yearning hipways—
    not those knees;
    they are a room apart.
But there is a kind of knee
that gropes with mind and eye
across a space
across the boundaries
which separate strangers
recognize.

          And when these knees touch,
as ours did just now,
there is no need
for hands exploring
    over indeterminate bulge
    and layers of frustration,
no need to question.

We will meet.
And then our knees
    of mind and eye
    and all our joints and angles
will curve together
momentarily maybe
as we remember that moment when
our knees touched.

THESEUS AT MIDNIGHT

Sacrifice myself to your Procrustean bed
And should I condescend?
You so unwittingly
Temper me between those sheets
That I upon awaking
Find unwonted changes
(though you are unaware
of their conception).
Should it be mine to make the change?
Should it be mine to arrange
I'd share the name of outlaw too
And make you sleep there.
Mine to arrange
And mine to share
Beneath the dream's persistent canopy
And I surpass my goal;
I seek it still.
Alarmed abruptly to awareness
I must choose
Between the two: sacrifice myself
Or you.

MAKE MUCH OF MOMENTS

Make much of moments; an action that precedes
The climax best fulfills
The need that prompts pursuit.
Anticipation measures satisfaction
Before completion of the act.

Dogs chase cars in hot pursuit
But never catch them; satisfaction
Comes through the chase, fulfills
Their primordial need to act.
Their ancestral role precedes.

The climax in music or in bed fulfills
A need but is minor to the act,
The ending only. Real satisfaction
Comes through suspense, uncertainty, and precedes
The anticlimactic end of the pursuit.

All joy, ephemeral at best, precedes
Finality, the end of satisfaction,
And then begins anew pursuit
Of accomplishments, and in this act
Comes realization of what fulfills.

A goal is reached with satisfaction
And both are finished. Pursuit
Alone provides the challenge of the act,

Excitement, pleasure, all of which precede
The denouement, all of which fulfill.

Satisfaction precedes the act; pursuit fulfills.

EPITHALAMIUM

Sing the nightly
Long awaited
Arrival of the nuptial hour
Anticipated
Brightly wreathed
In smiles and laughing
Eyes or blushing cheeks
And shy advances
Celebrated lightly
High with
Champagne flowing
And new-found friend
Acquainted slightly
May it never end.
Lie there now
Receptive, giving,
Reliving memories
Of how two met
Circulating
At a party, hoping
They could get together,
Groping for an answer
In smoke-filled room
And interminable chatter,
Choosing, losing
Interest in all others
Equally available
And attractive,

Then retiring
To find in faith
A lasting friendship
That, beginning now,
Might go on forever.
Lie there, arms
Enfolding, holding
On to dreams
Now celebrated
With the coupling
Of two lives and bodies,
Accomplishing an act
Somewhat overrated.

THRENODY

Glared the rudely
Watched and timed
Arrival of the closing hour
Expected to the minute
Shocking still
In gaunt revealing
Line and pale
Or sagging eye and
Thinning hair. Reflected
Neon glowed no more
Blue invitation hawking
Bottled respite or on tap.
Sat there then in smoke
On forehead hand
With empty glass
And upturned thoughts
Upon the checkered cloth
Alone and smelling
Of a broken love
To nibble at a pretzel heart
Ruminating drunk
Unwanted beer
Through smoke rings
Fast expanding
To a cloudy atmosphere
And visioned
In their curling density
A softened scene

A jukebox song
Screaming then as now
The unmatched fates
Of two who met
And loved. Memory turned
To mild pursuit
A first success first hot
And then enchantment gone
A cold response
Then none. Sat there
Holding glass and time
And tears in check
Till reminded of the law
And ushered out the door.

REUNION

When after years we met
as men retiring, shy
we shook and smiled appraising
aware at once of years
and samenesses.

Was it really you?
The triteness striking,
we couldn't say how
little we had changed,
the evidence before us.

Returning now
to Bennet's Grove, named jejunely
for a University football player,
for interminable coffees
as once, before we shared,
completely, the basement
behind the graduate school,
we found it noisy
and not private.

We went back an hour
reliving lavished love
when that was all we had,
remembering behind our eyes,
avoiding mention of it all—
now spent.

Kukla you had called me
from the Russian.
Muñeca from the Spanish (I
have used the name
once since) and now we both
remembered, but the words
fell dead.

Too soon,
too soon you had to go
perhaps to the Ideal
to regain more past
(Nick, bartender, host,
who couldn't read
the classical Greek
we brought him,
is dead) and I,
I just sitting here
stirring coffee
cold as upturned memories,
turn inward.

TANTUM ERGO

We create our oceans,
Delicately selecting
Our blend of hues and textures
To suit our moods, our needs
Leading us to choose
What depths, what shallows,
What paths to navigate,
What harbors we will use.

We build our ships,
Carefully incorporating
Our keels of comfort and holds
To accommodate our longings,
Topsides decked and trim
Enshrouded in mystery and confidence
That our vessels buoy us up,
Shipshape stern to stem.

INSCRIPTIONS

Inscriptions of lost lovers
Disintegrate to trackless beach
As sands dry
Gulls claw
Waves wash in
Merciless conspiracy
Against inscriptions.

Words
Too sentimental to repeat
Too ordinary to recall,
Ritualistic primitive chants
As John loves Mary,
Work-accomplished
Fatal messages, unsaid
Have shared those fates
Which these destructions
Leave untold.

GULLS

Early birds catching the warm
Rays of the young sun, light
On illusions, imaginations
Racing, outdistancing reality.

Decked out to cover
Their bulging indulgences
They waddle or perch on the edge
Of a tide ever ebbing beneath burning
Light, and feathers are shed
Under the welcome sun worshipping
Fancy flights, flirting with desuetude.

Seeking to gain, to preserve
What memories serve inaccurately,
They claw their ways among accretions,
Smells of the dying, shells of the dead,
Under the swelling rays as the sun
Flies high over expectations.

They vie against gravity
Matching accomplishments,
Competition stronger as the day
Grows old. Heavily leaning
On the horizon, the sagging sun
Slants resignation as they
Harbor an emptiness
After their hard day's sunning.

SNAILS

Converging on sands flattened by routine
and change, they emerge from their commonplaces
   and
wrapped in their egos against threatened rejection,
their bravado against isolation, they wander
or wade tides' slender margins, wrapped
in their vanity avoiding detection. Braving their ways
in sea weeds and shells, they seek the acceptable,
offer themselves, wrapped in their nudity
against observation, naively fearing exposure.

SHOREBIRDS

In morning warming shine on shallows
And fish filled watery dream fulfilling pose,
Patiently they wait to play their game, minnows
And shorebirds, with whatever eddies and undertows
Wash into the sharp-eyed focus of these aficionadoes,
These fancy flighted anglers of fin-filled billows.

TRANQUILITY

In this pool I can see
More worlds than my own
With the sky as high
As the trees grown deep
Into the burnished water
Alive at its level
With ripples and insects.
Above, gentle airs—
Bouquets on breezes—
Mix with the whispers
Of needles and leaves,
And peace is repeated
Down deep where a turtle
Aims lazily, gracefully,
Edging its way through
My three-way world
Wrapped into one
Of reflection.

THE HOUSE ON FOREST

Here is the house where I lived
Still as it was, I suppose, large, set back,
Except that all memory and imagination
Have lodged since I left for colleges and wars
There in the little room at the head of the stairs
Where Poe sits pondering weak and from those dark
    trees
Comes the bird, an owl actually,
Which we captured and kept in the coop behind
And Hamlet jests with Yorick my brother
As they stalk starlings with an old .22
And won't bid me shoot or
My sister pampers her pet in the parlor
Where we practiced piano, surprising each other with
    Haydn
While Samsa ages in the adjoining room
Through whose windows Miss Jessel can tussle for
    innocence
But Miles my young brother is safely inside,
And there with orchard for a dome,
The vineyard where the grapes are rather soured
Because Nero my cousin and I burned them
And hid in the barn playing an ancient Victrola,
But it's the house, the house, where
Stalks el Capitaneo, swaggart braggadocio
With the last (and only) Duchess my mother
As they together descend the stairs
And look through pillars towards the light
Which in the dark street meets hopes
And fears tonight.

SMALL CATS

They stalk their jungle prey
On tailored grass,
Crouch by hedges
Neat as gardens,
Wait,
Anticipate the passing
Of a small gazelle
Shadowed by a shrub
Then leap
And sink their needle claws into
The flesh of emptiness
And tussle with it
Rolling on the well-sown grass.
They hem high hedges
Hunting under surge of sky
And sharkskin sun their
Antelopes or ants
And, frightened by a spider,
Spring away and come to rest
On clipped and scissored lawn
And grasses smoothly pressed.

THINGS REMEMBERED

The child enfolded
In his skin alone
Against experiences:
Hunger, love intruding
On his daily need for gain,
Rebels at changes,
Knowing only life
Among familiarities: his blocks,
Of all his cherished toys,
Arranged to give
A double view
Of how a building looks to him,
A vision of a world to build.

This child of two
Begins to suffer shocks
As when, in changing homes,
His blocks are spilled
In transit;
Blocks go tumbling down
Along with knowledge
Of a never-changing world.

To carefree days,
Contentment, joy,
Belong his faintest recollections;
Pleasures fade compared to upsets—
Making wrong decisions,

Guilt inflicted, fault denied
By parents whose religion
Separates their world
From nature,
His from God.

Events recalled impress
By what excites or hurts—
By Joe E. Brown *The Circus Clown*
Attended with his cousin—
Two white rats
Escaping in the couch
To frighten one who comes to visit—
Reprimands for deeds detected,
Punishments for having fun.

LULLABY TO A FRIEND

Regard the world, the room
from where pendant on my lap
and purring, you continue to pursue
adventures of a busy day, and
as my fingers gently probe
behind your ear and under chin,
satisfied with softness, go to sleep.
To sleep, to dream
of all your day's accomplishments—
an errant ant annoyed, a bird
seen and sought, but
as your persistent twitching indicates,
not seized. Do
visions of lost lizards
course through your dream
and as your tiny claw distends
do they meet their satisfying ends?
Dream on, drowsy, soothed
by warmth and fondle. Turmoil cease.
Perhaps, my friend, tonight, like yours,
My sleep will bring such untormented peace.

LULLABY

Tiny, perfect, wave goodnight,
Little wrinkled fingers curled
Around the innocence of days,
The purity of slumber.

Tiny, perfect, silent now,
Little lips that sought the breast,
Satisfied, relax to form
The purity of kisses.

Tiny, perfect, eyelids close
On little worlds untouched by cares.
The fleeting frown smoothes out to show
The purity of dreaming.

THE WAKE

What gentle passing creates a wave
To inundate the shore? Who fear
The water lapping make a grave

Mistake. The lake is deep and clear
Reflecting beauty being part
Of it, and when the waves expire

At water's edge, they splash there not
To fade but spread their beauty where
It never ends nor joys depart.

A LIFE IN THE DAY

I.
Turn once more
In lumpy bed of dark
Give way to dawn
Rumpled sheets
And covers all
Forgetful now
Of threatened ills
That darkling dawn
Irons out. Renew
Geronto-neoteric pursuance
Preconceived in dreams
And waking fancies
Unaware or careless
That their inkling persistency
Confuses demarcation
Between reality and thought.
Withdraw. Abandon
Unknown origins
Unfathomably remote
Primordial haunts, claims
Significant and surfacing
Awake. Let inching light
Mete out on morning
Sill approaching hours
Regenerative. Premeditate
Events of moment and
Inconsequence stretching
New horizons beneath

Old skies promising newness
Now. Arise.

II.
Unfurl before our faithless
Innocency, our youthfulness
Untrammeled in pristine pregnability,
Order to assume, escutcheons
Blotless. We would be led
And yet too easily we err,
Learning young only to forget
About aggressiveness in our world
Of boundaries not to be transgressed
But often are. We learn young,
Too soon capitulating to forces
Once eschewed with innocent instinct,
Infused in dimmest infancy,
Dim instinctive warnings that neglected
Upset what we learn young
And then too soon forget—
That virtue is invention
Inheritable as vice. Make morning
Light inaugural, splendent with utility
And grace that attenuates our faith,
Replaces it with understanding, alleviates
Dependence, elevates.

III.
Now easily-abroad warming forces
Burgeoned worlds renewed
Of leaf and flower with young, original

Creations repeated from a pattern.
Establish these. Shine or shower down
Regeneratively enrichments, benedictions
That from seedling sentience
May myriads mature. Nurture now
What husbands and shepherds best
Fledgling and immature moments
Growing slowly into gathering hours
When present endeavors' recompense
Outproportions input, and labor
Accomplishes a name. Following
Risks of initial investment, pain,
Bestow with stimulant vigor adequate
Unfoldment, increase. Balance against
All losses, gain.

IV.
With sun-high semisatisfaction in
Commitments half fulfilled take time.
Take time considering weaknesses,
Fatigue warranting respite
Considering hunger, accomplishment
Already met or yet to be assigned.
Weaknesses gain strength
From repast, and fatigue
Gives way to repletion
With energy restored. Warrant amply
Wants and wishes now against
Post meridiem accomplishments promised
Following rest refreshed

With minds alive, bodies strong,
And appetites suppressed.

V.
Hanging on hands weary of demands
Apprehended, consigned, discharged—the mind
Westering with the sun—time has heavily begun
Eroding slowly resolutions partly, wholly.
Seconds or minutes drag as spirits dip and sag.
Homeward glance shifts surreptitiously askance
At watched and timed arriving of the hour, contriving
To look occupied. Through afternoon, release denied
Till accomplishments that compete with time are
    complete
Enough to show attainment of a beneficial gain.

VI.
As the hours of this day have produced
A lovely one
And more days come, are ever present,
It naturally unfolds that tomorrow, as today,
Will likewise be fulfilled, complete.
Conscience is virtue, necessity already met,
And accomplishment seen in attainment.
Hazards of indolence, truancy, acquisitiveness,
All other attractions, may be eschewed
For days provide light, growth, gain, strength,
    substance,
And remain the same for ever and ever.

VII.

Retire now to couch
With cursory contemplation
Dwindling failure or
Fulfillment satisfied
With momentary present passion
And release from
Entanglement and joy.
Lie long and languid
Under cover contour
Outlined only, dusk to dawn
Light lying safe at edges—
All other threatens, harms.
Obliterate illuminance and rest,
Assured that darkness
Blind, opaque, impenetrable,
Brooks no breach,
Abolishes possible evil
And guilt. Release
Responsibility and care
Insouciantly for nothing
But quiescence
Nestled in relief of
Blanket blackness
To fall eventually asleep.
Relinquish all.

Poems stand by themselves. Explanations insult by telling readers what they should think. Poetry should be symbols with meanings left open-ended, not similes which supply both ends of comparisons. "Pursuit of the Whole," for instance, becomes one extended metaphor of first contacts with academia, impressions of my first year at U. of M. in Ann Arbor, condensed into its present form some years later. That is history, not explanation. Meanings in poetry lie with its readers just as in all works of art: symbols, open to whatever interpretations might be suggested to those who perceive them.

Indeed, many of these poems stem from reactions to works of art. I once drove to Chicago specifically to see El Greco's *St. Martin and the Beggar* which became inspiration for my poem with that title. I have seen few actual pictures upon which my poems are built although visits to MOMA in New York, The Tate in London, Gustave Moreau Museum in Paris helped with such poems as "Liberation," "Ennui," and "Fate and the Angel of Death.' I own Marcia McGrath's "El Sembrador." *The Christian Science Monitor*'s Home Forum page printed photographs of works by Enoch Wood Perry, Ferdinand Hodler, and Russell Redmond, in which I found inspiration for "The True American," "The Disillusioned," and "Tantum Ergo."

I do not seek to find artists' meanings necessarily; often my ideas run counter to what an artist intended as is certainly the case with "Terrorism," based on Jack

Levine's *The Spanish Prison*. "Siren Song" uses Max Ernst's title *When Sirens Awake Reason Goes to Sleep* combined with Chad Walsh's recently devised poetical form: *quintina*. "Make Much of Moments" employs this same form.

Certainly Christo, whose white-panelled *Running Fence* stretched across Sonoma and Marin counties in California for four years before being torn down, would not object to my reaction to his work, nor would Ben Shahn find much fault in my interpretations of three of his pictures in "Liberation," "The Dispossessed," and "The Lucky Dragon."

Those familiar with Lafcadio Hearn's translation of *The Temptation of Saint Anthony* might catch familiar glimpses in five excerpts from my full-length version. My poems are reworkings, not translations, tailored to fit my philosophy. Several of these poems began with Redon, rather than Flaubert. I do not eschew borrowing, however, in small ways. Marianne Moore (whose poems are full of borrowings), Virginia Woolf, Havelock Ellis, Montagu Slater, Robert Frost, Emily Dickinson, Shakespeare, the Bible, plus Flaubert, all figure in these poems.

Nearly thirty of these poems relate directly to works by artists as disparate as Walter Sickert, Georges Rouault, Francis Bacon, Max Oppenheimer, Anton Lehmden, and Yossel Berger. Those that have been published have stood by themselves independent of the works that inspired them. I am grateful to Emily McCormick, editor of FORMS—The Review of Anthroporos Theophoros, Ruth G. Iodice of *Blue Unicorn*, Menke Katz of *Bitterroot*, and Rod Walker of *Erehwon* for their help plus, of course, for their having published so many of these poems.